PREHISTORIC WORLD

THE AGE OF MAMMALS

Dougal Dixon

BARRON'S

First edition for the United States, its territories and dependencies, Canada, and
the Philippine Republic published in 2006 by Barron's Educational Series, Inc.

Copyright © 2006 *ticktock* Entertainment Ltd. First published in Great Britain by ticktock Media Ltd.

All inquiries should be addressed to:
Barron's Educational Series, Inc.
250 Wireless Blvd.
Hauppauge, New York 11788
www.barronseduc.com

Library of Congress Control Number: 2005938246

ISBN-13: 978-0-7641-3480-7
ISBN-10: 0-7641-3480-9

Printed in China
9 8 7 6 5 4 3 2 1

CONTENTS

INTRODUCTION

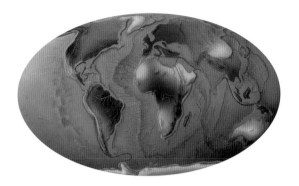

This map shows how the Earth looked at the end of the Tertiary Period. As the continents moved, the landscape changed and new animals evolved.

This map shows how the Earth looks today. The continents are in similar positions, but they are closer together than they were in Tertiary times.

Prehistoric World is a series of six books about the evolution of animals.

The Earth's history is divided into sections called periods. These periods last millions of years. Each book in this series looks at the most important periods in prehistory.

This book looks at the Tertiary Period. During this time, huge open plains of grass formed. Mammals developed long legs to suit this new environment.

PREHISTORIC WORLD TIMELINE

Use this timeline to trace prehistoric life. It shows how simple creatures evolved into more different kinds. This took millions and millions of years. That is what MYA stands for – millions of years ago.

	BOOK	PERIOD	
CENOZOIC ERA	**THE ICE AGE**	1.75 MYA to now QUATERNARY	*This is a period of ice ages and mammals. Our direct relatives, Homo sapiens, also appear.*
	ANCIENT MAMMALS	65 to 1.75 MYA TERTIARY	*Giant mammals and huge, hunting birds appear in this period. Our first human relatives also start to evolve.*
MESOZOIC ERA	**CRETACEOUS LIFE**	135 to 65 MYA CRETACEOUS	*Huge dinosaurs evolve. They all die by the end of this period.*
	JURASSIC LIFE	203 to 135 MYA JURASSIC	*Large and small dinosaurs and flying creatures develop.*
	TRIASSIC LIFE	250 to 203 MYA TRIASSIC	*The "Age of Dinosaurs" begins. Mammals also start to appear.*
PALEOZOIC ERA	**EARLY LIFE**	295 to 250 MYA PERMIAN	*Sail-backed reptiles start to appear.*
		355 to 295 MYA CARBONIFEROUS	*The first reptiles appear, and tropical forests develop.*
		410 to 355 MYA DEVONIAN	*Bony fish evolve. Trees and insects appear.*
		435 to 410 MYA SILURIAN	*Fish with jaws develop, and land creatures appear.*
		500 to 435 MYA ORDOVICIAN	*Primitive fishes, trilobites, shellfish, and plants evolve.*
		540 to 500 MYA CAMBRIAN	*First animals with skeletons appear.*

MEGISTOTHERIUM

Before the evolution of modern carnivores, such as lions and bears, there was a group of predators called the creodonts. *Megistotherium* was the biggest of these, with a skull twice as long as a tiger's. It might have been the largest hunting land mammal that has ever lived.

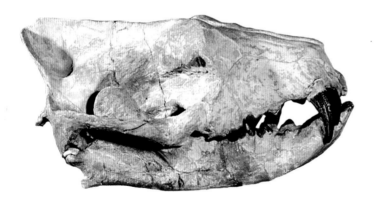

This is the skull of a creodont. Not all creodonts were as big as *Megistotherium* – some were only the size of a weasel. But all creodonts were fierce hunters, with powerful jaws and great bone-crushing, meat-ripping teeth.

ANIMAL
FACTFILE

NAME: *Megistotherium* (the biggest beast)

PRONOUNCED: meh-jiss-toe-theer-ee-um

GROUP: Creodont mammal

WHERE IT LIVED: North Africa

WHEN IT LIVED: Mid Tertiary Period (50 to 20 million years ago)

LENGTH: 15.75 feet (4.8 meters)

SPECIAL FEATURES: The biggest meat-eating land mammal known

FOOD: Big animals like elephants

MAIN ENEMY: None

DID YOU KNOW?: Only a single complete skull of *Megistotherium* has been found, although small pieces of other skulls have been discovered.

With a head that measured about 4 feet (1.2 meters) long, and a body that must have been the size of a bison, *Megistotherium* was big enough, powerful enough and fierce enough to hunt and eat elephants!

Moropus

Scientists can tell how an animal lived by looking at the shape of its skeleton. The head of *Moropus* was like that of a horse. This tells us that it was a plant-eating animal. Its front legs were longer than its hind legs, like a giraffe. This tells us that it could stretch its neck upwards rather than feed from the ground. So this was an animal that must have fed from high branches.

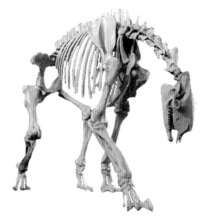

At first glance you would think that the skeleton of *Moropus* is that of a horse. In fact it was a close relative although it had claws instead of hooves.

NAME: *Moropus* (slow foot)

PRONOUNCED: mawr-oh-pus

GROUP: Chalicothere family
of perissodactyls

WHERE IT LIVED: North America

WHEN IT LIVED: Mid to Late Tertiary
Period (23 to 14 million years ago)

HEIGHT: 7.8 feet (2.4 meters) at
the shoulder

SPECIAL FEATURES: Big claws
for ripping down vegetation

FOOD: Leaves

MAIN ENEMY: Big meat-eating
mammals like *Amphicyon*

DID YOU KNOW?: When
paleontologists first found the
Moropus claws, they thought they
must have come from a giant sloth.

Moropus used its big claws
to reach up and pull down
branches so that it could
feed on the leaves that grew
high up in trees. There
were several members of
this chalicothere group,
but *Moropus* was the biggest.

PYROTHERIUM

For most of the Tertiary Period, South America was separated from North America by sea. Different mammals evolved in South America because it was an island. Some animals looked like those that lived on other continents, but they were not related. *Pyrotherium* looked like an elephant.

Male *Pyrotherium* may have used their tusks and trunks to fight with one another to decide who was going to mate with the females.

With its tusks and trunk, *Pyrotherium* must have looked like an elephant. It may have lived like one too, digging in the ground with its tusks, and picking up food with its short trunk.

ANIMAL FACTFILE

NAME: *Pyrotherium* (fire mammal, because its fossils were found near a volcano)

PRONOUNCED: pi-ro-theer-ee-um

GROUP: Pyrothere group of the xenungulates — the "foreign hoofed mammals"

WHERE IT LIVED: Bolivia and Argentina

WHEN IT LIVED: Mid Tertiary Period (29 to 23 million years ago)

LENGTH: 8.8 feet (2.7 meters)

SPECIAL FEATURES: Heavy animal with a trunk and tusks

FOOD: Plants

MAIN ENEMY: Big meat-eating marsupials

DID YOU KNOW?: *Pyrotherium* was such a mixture of different kinds of animal that it is difficult to tell what it is related to. It had the tusks and trunk of an elephant, teeth like a hippopotamus, and the ear bones of a hoofed mammal.

*U*INTATHERIUM

The *Uintatherium* may have looked like a rhinoceros, with a big heavy body and horns, but they were not related. Many rhinoceros-like mammals lived in early Tertiary times. They probably evolved to take the place of horned dinosaurs like *Triceratops*, that had only just become extinct.

Uintatherium weighed something like two tons, and carried itself on massive elephant-like legs. It was probably only the males that had the 3 feet (1 meter) long tusks. They may have used them to attract or scare other animals.

Uintatherium must have looked very frightening. It had six horns on its head and a pair of sharp tusks in its upper jaw. However, it was probably a slow-witted plant-eater.

ANIMAL
FACTFILE

NAME: *Uintatherium* (mammal from the Uinta Mountains in the U.S.)

PRONOUNCED: you-in-ta-theer-ee-um

GROUP: Uintathere

WHERE IT LIVED: Utah

WHEN IT LIVED: Early Tertiary Period (40 to 35 million years ago)

LENGTH: 13 feet (4 meters)

SPECIAL FEATURES: Three pairs of horns and a pair of sharp tusks

FOOD: Plants

MAIN ENEMY: None

DID YOU KNOW?: In the 1870s two American palaeontologists, Othniel Marsh and Edward Cope, argued bitterly over who should name this animal. It was finally named *Uintatherium* by another paleontologist, Joseph Leidy, in 1872.

MEGACEROPS

In the early part of the Tertiary Period there were many rhinoceros-shaped mammals. One group of these were called the brontotheres, and they ranged from little animals no bigger than a rabbit, to huge beasts like *Megacerops*, which was bigger than an elephant.

Despite the size of the skull, *Megacerops* had a small brain – smaller in proportion than that of most dinosaurs.

The horns of *Megacerops* and the other brontotheres were not true horns at all. They were bony lumps that were probably covered by skin, like giraffe "horns."

ANIMAL FACTFILE

NAME: *Megacerops* (big horned head)

PRONOUNCED: meg-ah-sair-ops

GROUP: Brontothere (thunder mammal)

WHERE IT LIVED: Western North America

WHEN IT LIVED: Early Tertiary Period (58 to 30 million years ago)

LENGTH: over 13 feet (4 meters) long and 7.8 feet (2.4 meters) high at the shoulder

SPECIAL FEATURES: Massive nose decoration that was shaped like the letter Y

FOOD: Low-growing vegetation

MAIN ENEMY: Big meat-eating mammals such as creodonts

DID YOU KNOW?: Scientists think that only male *Megacerops* had a nose decoration, and it was used to attract females. This suggests that *Megacerops* lived in large herds.

INDRICOTHERIUM

This massive beast is an ancient relative of the rhinoceros. Unlike modern rhinoceroses, it did not have a horn on its nose. An animal this size would not need a weapon to defend itself. It is the biggest known land mammal ever to have lived.

As can be seen from this fossil, the *Indricotherium* had two pairs of teeth at the front of the mouth. It also had two tusk-like teeth on the upper jaw that pointed downward and two on the lower jaw that pointed forward. Together they were used for scraping leaves and twigs from high branches to eat.

ANIMAL
FACTFILE

NAME: *Indricotherium* (mammal of Indrik — a monster of local legends)

PRONOUNCED: in-drik-oh-theer-ee-um

GROUP: Perissodactyl (odd-toed hoofed mammals)

WHERE IT LIVED: Pakistan

WHEN IT LIVED: Mid-Tertiary Period (20 to 30 million years ago)

LENGTH: 26.2 feet (8 meters) long, and 14.75 feet (4.5 meters) tall at the shoulder. An elephant is about 23 feet (7 meters) long and 10 feet (3 meters) tall at the shoulder

SPECIAL FEATURES: The biggest land mammal that we know of

FOOD: Leaves and twigs

MAIN ENEMY: None

DID YOU KNOW?: *Indricotherium* must have weighed about 10 tons.

Although *Indricotherium* was like a rhinoceros, it lived more like a giraffe. Its long legs, on three-toed feet, held its body high above the ground. The tall neck and the head (which was over 3 feet [1 meter] long) reached to the tops of the highest trees.

BASILOSAURUS

One of the earliest whales was *Basilosaurus*. Like all whales, it was a mammal. Although mammals evolved on land, many of them returned to the sea at the beginning of the Tertiary Period. The giant sea reptiles had become extinct, and sea-living mammals evolved to take their place.

Like the whales of today, *Basilosaurus* would have needed to come to the surface to breathe. It had nostrils at the tip of its nose, rather than a blowhole on top of its head as modern whales do.

ANIMAL
FACTFILE

NAME: *Basilosaurus* (emperor lizard)

PRONOUNCED: bass-il-oh-sawr-us

GROUP: Archaeocete whale

WHERE IT LIVED: All the oceans

WHEN IT LIVED: Early Tertiary Period (45 to 35 million years ago)

LENGTH: 60 feet (18 meters)

SPECIAL FEATURES: A long, thin and flexible body, ideal for catching fish

FOOD: Fish and cephalopods

MAIN ENEMY: Maybe sharks

DID YOU KNOW?: Although it is a mammal, *Basilosaurus* has a name like a dinosaur. This is because the first scientist to find its fossils thought that they came from a giant reptile.

This fossil shows the long, snake-like backbone of *Basilosaurus*. Over a hundred years ago, someone stuck several bones together from different skeleteons and tried to pass it off as a sea serpent.

DESMOSTYLUS

This hippopotamus-like animal with strange crooked legs lived around the edge of the Pacific Ocean in mid-Tertiary times. It probably used its tusks and heavy teeth to root about on the shallow sea floor for shellfish, or perhaps it grazed on seaweeds. It was such an odd animal that scientists are not sure what it ate!

This is a fossil of *Desmostylus'* teeth. From the chemicals in its bones, scientists have worked out that it spent most of its time in water – by the shore or in river mouths.

ANIMAL
FACTFILE

NAME: *Desmostylus* (chain-tooth, after the way the back teeth are linked together)

PRONOUNCED: des-mo-sty-lus

GROUP: Desmostylid mammal

WHERE IT LIVED: Coasts of Japan and California

WHEN IT LIVED: Mid to Late Tertiary Period (14 to 19 million years ago)

LENGTH: 5.9 feet (1.8 meters)

SPECIAL FEATURES: A lumbering semi-aquatic mammal with powerful teeth

FOOD: Shellfish or seaweed

MAIN ENEMY: Sharks

DID YOU KNOW?: The nearest living relative of *Desmostylus* is the elephant.

The inwardly-turned feet of *Desmostylus* made it very clumsy while walking on land. Underwater, though, it would have been very graceful. It could walk across the sea bed as a hippopotamus does in African rivers today.

GOMPHOTHERIUM

Elephants existed for most of the Tertiary Period. They started as small pig-like animals, but soon developed into big beasts with tusks and trunks. Many types of elephants evolved with different arrangements of tusks. *Gomphotherium* was an elephant with four tusks.

The tusks on the lower jaw of *Gomphotherium* made the jaw very long and spade-like. The tusks could have been used for rooting in the forest floor, or in the beds of streams and lakes looking for food.

We do not know for sure if *Gomphotherium* had a trunk because trunks are made of flesh that does not fossilize. However, the short neck shows that the head could not reach the ground, and the skull shows features similar to the trunk area of modern elephants. As a result, scientists think the *Gomphotherium* probably had a trunk.

ANIMAL FACTFILE

NAME: *Gomphotherium* (bolted mammal)

PRONOUNCED: gomp-foe-theer-ee-um

GROUP: Elephant

WHERE IT LIVED: Europe, Kenya, Pakistan, Japan, and North America

WHEN IT LIVED: Late Tertiary Period (23 to 3 million years ago)

LENGTH: 13 feet (4 meters)

SPECIAL FEATURES: Elephant with a pair of tusks on the upper jaw and another on the lower

FOOD: Plants

MAIN ENEMY: None

DID YOU KNOW?: *Gomphotherium* probably evolved in Africa and then spread to the rest of the world.

DEINOTHERIUM

Modern elephants have their tusks on the upper jaw. *Deinotherium* had its tusks on the lower jaw and they turned downwards. These tusks could have been used as picks for digging up roots and other ground vegetation.

Deinotherium is one of largest land animals known. It existed for almost 20 million years – a very long time.

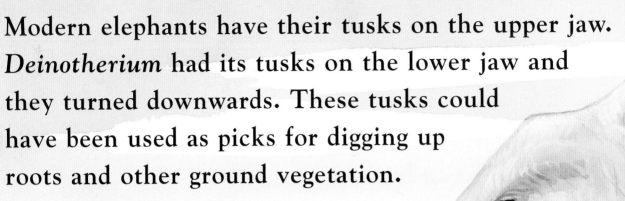

The early discovery of *Deinotherium* skulls on the Greek Islands may have led to the legend of the Cyclops – the one-eyed giant. The nostrils in the skull are fused into a single hole, which looks like an enormous eye socket.

ANIMAL FACTFILE

NAME: *Deinotherium* (terrible mammal)

PRONOUNCED: dy-no-theer-ee-um

GROUP: Elephant

WHERE IT LIVED: Africa and Southern Europe

WHEN IT LIVED: Late Tertiary Period (20 to 2 million years ago)

HEIGHT: 13 feet (4 meters) at the shoulders

SPECIAL FEATURES: Down-curved tusks on the lower jaw

FOOD: Plants

MAIN ENEMY: None

DID YOU KNOW?: *Deinotherium* was around at the same time as our earliest human ancestors.

SIVATHERIUM

Sivatherium had horns, and looked like a moose, but it was really a kind of a giraffe. It was not the long-necked, long-legged animal that we know today, but a heavily built browsing animal. It probably had a muscular upper lip, like the long nose of a moose.

Today there are only two types of giraffe – the long-necked giraffe of the African plains and the short-necked okapi of the forests. In Tertiary times there were dozens of different types.

We can imagine the huge, branching horns of *Sivatherium* by looking at a moose. *Sivatherium* had two pairs of horns, but only the back pair were like antlers. The pair in front were quite small.

ANIMAL FACTFILE

NAME: *Sivatherium* (mammal of Shiva – an Indian god)

PRONOUNCED: see-va-theer-ee-um

GROUP: Giraffe

WHERE IT LIVED: Africa and Asia

WHEN IT LIVED: Late Tertiary Period to the Early Quaternary Period (5 to 1 million years ago)

HEIGHT: 6.5 feet (2 meters) at the shoulder

SPECIAL FEATURES: Two pairs of horns on the head

FOOD: Plants

MAIN ENEMY: Lions and giant bears

DID YOU KNOW?: There are rock paintings of an animal that looks like *Sivatherium* in the Sahara Desert. It seems as if it survived long enough for early people to paint it.

AMPHICYON

Amphicyon was as big as a grizzly bear. It was one of the largest hunting animals in Middle Tertiary times. With its massive body and powerful legs it could hunt down most of the animals that were around, and kill them with its sharp dog-like teeth.

The legs of *Amphicyon* were short, and it walked on flat feet like a bear. It could not have run fast. It probably hunted its prey by ambushing it rather than running it down.

The *Amphicyon* is neither a bear nor a dog, but something in between. The amphicyonids were the main hunters of the Middle Tertiary, and ranged from the size of badgers to the size of the biggest bears.

ANIMAL FACTFILE

NAME: *Amphicyon* (nearly a dog)

PRONOUNCED: am-fee-sy-on

GROUP: Amphicyonid — the bear dogs

WHERE IT LIVED: Europe and North America

WHEN IT LIVED: Mid Tertiary Period (30 to 14 million years ago)

HEIGHT: 3 feet (1 meter)

SPECIAL FEATURES: Skeleton like that of a bear, but teeth like that of a dog

FOOD: Other animals, particularly the small horses of the time

MAIN ENEMY: None

DID YOU KNOW?: The bear-dogs took over from the creodonts in the early part of the Tertiary Period, and were then replaced by the canids (wolves, foxes, and dogs) in the later part.

ANIMAL FAMILIES GLOSSARY

Amphicyonid — the bear-dogs. These were meat-eating mammals from the Late Tertiary Period that were related both to the bears and the dogs.

Archaeocete — the earliest group of completely marine whales. They differed from modern whales and porpoises by having teeth of different shapes and sizes, with pointed snatching teeth at the front and meat-shearing teeth at the back.

Brontothere — a group of rhinoceros-like perissodactyls from the Early Tertiary Period. They ranged from the size of a pig to the size of an elephant.

Chalicothere — a perissodactyl group related to the horse. Instead of hooves they had big claws that would have been used for tearing down branches. They lived from Mid to Late Tertiary.

Creodont — a group of early meat-eating mammals from the Early Tertiary. Although they resembled modern wolves, weasels, and bears, they were not related to them.

Desmostylid — a group of semi-aquatic mammals that lived around the Pacific ocean in Mid to Late Tertiary times. They probably fed on seaweed and shellfish.

Perissodactyl — the group of odd-toed hoofed mammals. Modern forms include the horse, the rhinoceros, and the tapir. They normally have either one or three toes on the foot. The other hoofed mammal group are the artiodactyls — the even-toed hoofed mammals, and these include the sheep, the goats, and the deer.

Pyrothere — a group of xenungulates that resembled the modern elephant although they were not closely related to elephants. They lived in South America in the mid-Tertiary Period.

Uintathere — a group of heavy, rhinoceros-like mammals from the Early Tertiary Period. They had several pairs of horn-like structures on the head and a pair of long tusks.

Xenungulate — a group of hoofed mammals that lived in South America during the Tertiary Period. They were not related to the hoofed mammals of the rest of the world but evolved independently.

LOSSARY

Adapted — changed to survive in a particular habitat or weather conditions.

Ambushing — lying in wait, out of sight, and then making a surprise attack.

Blowhole — a hole at the top of a whale's head that acts like its nostril. To breathe a whale comes to the surface of the water and blows air out of the hole and breathes air in. When the whale is underwater, a flap of skin covers the hole.

Browsing — feeding on grass or leaves.

Continents — the world's main land masses, such as Africa and Europe.

Evolution — changes or developments that happen to all forms of life over millions of years as a result of changes in the environment.

Evolve — to change or develop.

Extinct — an animal group which no longer exists.

Fossils — the remains of a prehistoric plant or animal that has been turned to rock.

Fossilized — to turn into a fossil.

Mammal — a warm-blooded animal which is covered in hair. The female gives birth to live young and produces milk from her own body to feed them.

Marsupials — an animal such as a kangaroo, which has a pouch on the front of its body in which it carries its young.

Moose — a type of deer from North America.

Paleontologist — a scientist who studies fossils.

Prehistory — a time before humans evolved.

Primitive — a very early stage in the development of a species.

Reptiles — cold-blooded, crawling, or creeping animals with a backbone.

River mouth — the place where a river flows into the sea.

Rock paintings — drawings made by our early ancestors millions of years ago .

Semi-aquatic — animals which spend a lot of time in water but which need air to breathe, for example, turtles, otters, and frogs.

Sloth — a very slow moving animal which lives in rainforests.

Tropics — hot, wet countries that are close to the equator.

Tusk — a long pointed tooth which grows outside of an animal's mouth.

INDEX

PICTURE CREDITS

T = top, B = bottom, R = right, L = left

Main image: 6-7, 10-11, 16-17, 20-21 Simon Mendez; 18-19 Luis Rey;
8-9, 12-13, 14-15, 22-23, 24-25, 26-27, 28-29 Chris Tomlin

4TL, 4TR, 5 (Cenozoic Era), 6, 8, 15, 19, 20, 23, 25 Ticktock Media archive; 5 (Mesozoic Era top, Paleozoic Era top) Simon Mendez; 5 (Mesozoic Era center, Paleozoic Era bottom) Luis Rey; 5 (Mesozoic Era bottom) Lisa Alderson; 11 Amherst College Museum of Natural History; 27, 29 Shutterstock; 13 The Natural History Museum, London; 16 Ria Novosti/Science Photo Library

Every effort has been made to trace the copyright holders and we apologize in advance for any unintentional omissions.
We would be pleased to insert the appropriate acknowledgment in any subsequent edition of this publication.